Wild About

ATVs

J. Poolos

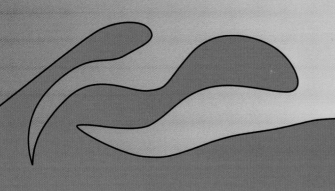

PowerKiDS
press.

New York

For Helena

Published in 2008 by The Rosen Publishing Group, Inc.
29 East 21st Street, New York, NY 10010

First Edition

Editor: Amelie von Zumbusch
Book Design: Greg Tucker
Photo Researcher: Nicole Pristash

Photo Credits: Cover, pp. 5, 9, 17 © Getty Images; pp. 7, 11, 13, 15, 19 © Shutterstock.com; p. 21 by Chuck DeBault.

Library of Congress Cataloging-in-Publication Data

Poolos, Jamie.
    Wild about ATVs / J. Poolos. — 1st ed.
        p. cm. — (Wild rides)
    Includes bibliographical references and index.
    ISBN-13: 978-1-4042-3793-3 (library binding)
    ISBN-10: 1-4042-3793-3 (library binding)
    1. All terrain vehicles—Juvenile literature. I. Title.
    TL235.6.P66 2008
    629.22'042—dc22
                                                        2007000930

Manufactured in the United States of America

Contents

ATVs on the Move

An all-terrain **vehicle** is a vehicle with an **engine** and big, strong wheels. All-terrain vehicles are called ATVs for short. They can have three, four, or six wheels. ATVs are used for both work and play. They are smaller than cars and trucks. They can travel through the woods and over mountains. ATVs can even cross small rivers!

Farmers, **ranchers**, U.S. park rangers, **rescue** teams, and other workers use ATVs. However, ATVs are also used for fun. People ride them on trails and over sand dunes, or hills. ATV racing is a popular, or well-liked, sport.

These ATV riders are part of a rescue team. They are coming back from saving a boy who was lost near Lily Lake, Utah.

How to Spot an ATV

ATVs come in many shapes and sizes. They can have either large or small engines. There are even small ATVs built for children. Some ATVs have three wheels. These ATVs are called trikes. There are also four-wheel ATVs, called quads. Both kinds of ATVs have big, fat tires. The tires help the ATV go over rocks and uneven ground.

All kinds of ATVs have seats and handlebars, just like motorcycles do. ATVs have narrow seats and wide handlebars that make them easy to control. ATVs also have lights so their riders can see at night.

The big tires on ATVs allow them to be driven through deep mud and on other uneven ground.

Any Number of Wheels

Some ATVs have six wheels. These ATVs are used mostly for work. Six-wheel ATVs sometimes have tools called dump boxes for carrying loads.

Three-wheel ATVs are used only for sport riding. They are easier to drive than four-wheel ATVs. However, three-wheel ATVs can be unsafe because they tip over easily. Four-wheel ATVs are by far the best-liked kind of ATV. They are easy to ride and hard to tip over. Four-wheel ATVs are excellent for children who are learning to ride. They are also great for **professional** ATV riders who ride them fast in races.

Some professional ATV riders like three-wheel ATVs, like this one, because they are lighter than quads.

The History of ATVs

The first three-wheel ATVs were made in 1970, by the motorcycle maker Honda. They had large, balloonlike tires, instead of **shock absorbers**, to go over the bumps. These ATVs were used for sport. In the 1980s, Honda put shock absorbers and smaller tires on its ATVs. It also added racks for carrying gear. Many hunters used these ATVs.

Later, Honda made a three-wheel ATV with a fast engine. However, three-wheel ATVs were thought to be unsafe because they tipped over easily. In 1983, a carmaker called Suzuki sold the first four-wheel ATV. Since then, four-wheel ATVs have become very popular.

Nearly all today's ATVs are four-wheel ATVs, like the one seen here.

ATV Makers and Their Vehicles

There are several different motorcycle and **snowmobile** makers that make ATVs. ATVs are made for both sport and utility, or work. The Yamaha YZF Raptor is one well-known sport ATV. Its powerful engine comes in sizes from 80cc to 660cc. The Suzuki Quadsport Z250 is a popular ATV for trail riding.

Motorcycle maker Kawasaki leads the way in the utility market with its Prairie 650. The Polaris Sportsman comes in a size for any rider. The company Arctic Cat also makes ATVs in all sizes. The farm company John Deere's Buck line of ATVs is a strong seller, too.

The lifeguards of Honolulu, Hawaii, use the Honda Fourtrax line of ATVs.

How to Ride an ATV

Riding an ATV takes much skill. However, even children can ride ATVs if they have training. First, you need the right gear. A **helmet** is the most important piece of gear. Next come strong boots. Racers wear padding that keeps their shoulders and legs safe. They wear gear called gloves on their hands.

Once you have your gear on, sit on the seat. Put your hands on the handlebars. Work the **throttle** with your right thumb. Your hands work the brake **levers**. Your right foot controls the brake **pedal**. To turn an ATV, push on the handlebar and lean into the turn.

Many ATV riders wear big glasses called goggles to keep the mud and wind out of their eyes.

Places to Ride an ATV

ATVs can travel over all kinds of ground. Many people like to ride them on forest trails. Some like to ride ATVs through large pits of mud, called mud bogs. Others like to ride on sand dunes, like those at Glamis, California. Still others like to ride in open fields. People who hunt and fish ride ATVs up mountains to reach far-off hunting grounds, lakes, or streams.

At ATV race tracks, people called stunt riders do tricks and put on shows for fans. Stunt riders often drive their ATVs off giant jumps and do tricks. Some can even do backflips!

This stunt rider is doing a trick at a show. Stunt drivers are very skilled and carefully trained.

The Race Is On!

Racers take their ATVs to tracks made of dirt or mud. The tracks have tight corners and long, straight parts, called straightaways. Many tracks have huge jumps.

Professional racers have teams of **mechanics** who travel with them from race to race. The mechanics make sure the ATVs are in good shape for the races. The race starts when someone drops a piece of cloth. The ATVs take off as fast as they can. The rider who takes the lead is said to have the "hole shot." The racers bump into each other as they fight for position.

There are ATV races for people who are not professionals, too. The people in this ATV race are seven- to ten-year-old kids!

19

Professional ATV Riders

There are a lot of great professional ATV racers. Most of them began riding ATVs when they were very young. Doug Gust is one well-known racer. He is the 2006 GNC champion, or winner. Gust is from Salem, Wisconsin. John Natalie, the 2005 GNC champion, is from Houtzdale, Pennsylvania. He won the Pro Quad Championship and the 12 Hours of ATV.

Joe Byrd is a racer from Union City, Tennessee. He has been racing for 19 years. He is the 2006 ATVA MX national champion. Byrd's wife, Amy, is a four-time GNC champion in the women's class.

John Natalie, seen here, took part in his first ATV race when he was just 12 years old.

ATVs by the Millions

Today there are **millions** of ATVs on trails, tracks, dunes, and farms. Sales of ATVs show no sign of slowing down. In fact, 780,433 ATVs were sold in 2005. That is a lot of ATVs!

Not everyone is happy about the growing number of ATVs, though. Some people worry that ATVs are bad for the **environment**. Environmental groups are calling for more control of ATVs. However, ATV groups are coming together to fight for their right to use ATVs on public land. No matter where people ride them, though, ATVs are likely to be popular for many years to come.

Glossary

engine (EN-jin) A machine inside a car or airplane that makes the car or airplane move.

environment (en-VY-ern-ment) All the living things of a place.

helmet (HEL-mit) A covering worn to keep the head safe.

levers (LEH-vurz) Rods that turns at a fixed point.

mechanics (mih-KA-niks) People who are skilled at fixing machines.

millions (MIL-yunz) A very large number.

pedal (PEH-dul) A tool that is pushed with a foot to make something work or move.

professional (pruh-FESH-nul) Someone who is paid for what he or she does.

ranchers (RAN-cherz) People who have large farms for raising cows, horses, or sheep.

rescue (RES-kyoo) Having to do with saving someone or something from danger.

shock absorbers (SHOK ub-SORB-erz) Things that make the object they are tied to shake less.

snowmobile (SNOH-moh-beel) A vehicle made to travel over the snow.

throttle (THRAH-tul) A handle that controls the supply of gas to an engine.

vehicle (VEE-uh-kul) A means of moving or carrying something.

Index

C
cars, 4

E
engine(s), 4, 6, 12
environment, 22

F
farmers, 4

H
helmet, 14

L
levers, 14

M
mechanics, 18
millions, 22
mountains, 4, 16

P
park rangers, 4
pedal, 14

R
races, 8, 18
ranchers, 4
rescue teams, 4
rivers, 4

S
shock absorbers, 10
snowmobile makers,
   12

T
throttle, 14
trucks, 4

V
vehicle, 4

W
wheels, 4, 6, 8
woods, 4

Web Sites

Due to the changing nature of Internet links, PowerKids Press has developed an online list of Web sites related to the subject of this book. This site is updated regularly. Please use this link to access the list: www.powerkidslinks.com/wild/atvs/

24